DATE DUE		

The Urbana Free Library

To renew: call 217-367-4057
or go to "*urbanafreelibrary.org*"
and select "Renew/Request Items"

FRESHWATER FISHING

BY SARA GREEN

BELLWETHER MEDIA • MINNEAPOLIS, MN

Jump into the cockpit and take flight with Pilot books. Your journey will take you on high-energy adventures as you learn about all that is wild, weird, fascinating, and fun!

This edition first published in 2013 by Bellwether Media, Inc.

No part of this publication may be reproduced in whole or in part without written permission of the publisher. For information regarding permission, write to Bellwether Media, Inc., Attention: Permissions Department, 5357 Penn Avenue South, Minneapolis, MN 55419.

Library of Congress Cataloging-in-Publication Data

Green, Sara, 1964-
Freshwater fishing / by Sara Green.
    p. cm. – (Pilot books: outdoor adventures)
Includes bibliographical references and index.
 Summary: "Engaging images accompany information about freshwater fishing. The combination of high-interest subject matter and narrative text is intended for students in grades 3 through 7"–Provided by publisher.
ISBN 978-1-60014-799-9 (hardcover : alk. paper)
 1. Fishing–Juvenile literature. 2. Freshwater fishes–Juvenile literature. I. Title.
SH445.G74 2013
799.1'1–dc23
                            2012015708

Printed in the United States of America, North Mankato, MN.

TABLE OF CONTENTS

THE MORNING CATCH

The sun begins to rise above a misty **freshwater** lake. An **angler** steers his boat along the shore. He comes to some fallen trees and stops. This is a perfect place to find fish. He takes out a fishing rod and puts a worm on the hook. Then he **casts** the line out near the fallen trees.

After a few minutes, he feels a tug on the line. He **sets the hook** and hauls in a huge fish. It is a bass! The angler removes the hook from the fish's mouth and takes a picture. Then he releases the bass back into the lake. What a great way to start the day!

Freshwater fishing is the most popular kind of fishing in the United States. Anglers of all ages and skill levels enjoy fishing in the country's lakes, rivers, and streams. Even a small pond can have a surprising number of fish!

Catching Lunch

Many anglers eat the fish they catch. Most freshwater fish contain a lot of protein and little fat. They can be a healthy part of any meal.

People love the sport of fishing for different reasons. Some anglers simply enjoy being in nature on a quiet lake. Others like the challenge of finding, hooking, and **landing** a difficult fish. Many people fish to spend time outdoors with friends and family.

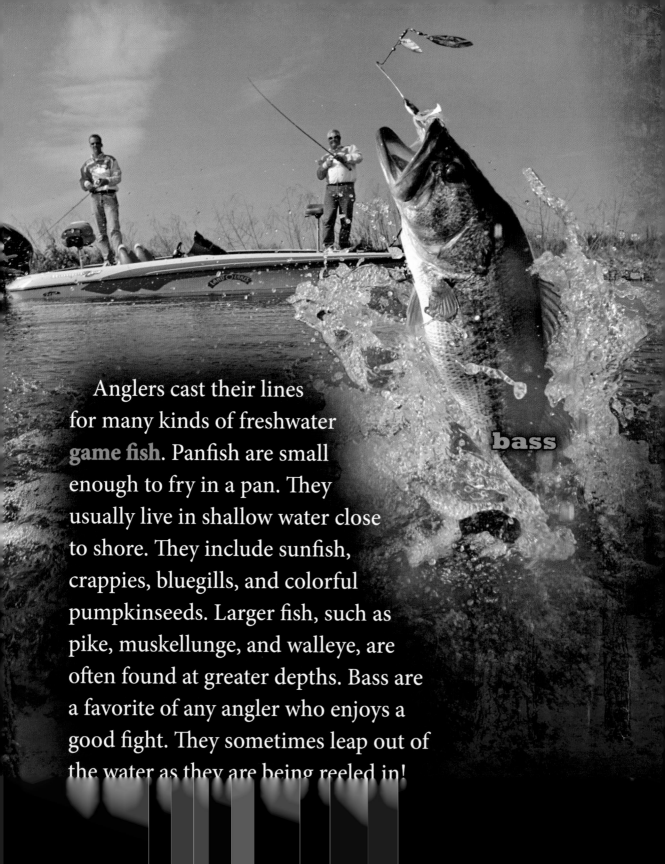

bass

Anglers cast their lines for many kinds of freshwater **game fish**. Panfish are small enough to fry in a pan. They usually live in shallow water close to shore. They include sunfish, crappies, bluegills, and colorful pumpkinseeds. Larger fish, such as pike, muskellunge, and walleye, are often found at greater depths. Bass are a favorite of any angler who enjoys a good fight. They sometimes leap out of the water as they are being reeled in!

Part of the excitement of freshwater fishing is locating good fishing spots. Fish often seek cover near docks, plants, fallen trees, or other objects in the water. Areas where birds are feeding on **baitfish** near the surface are also worth trying. Game fish are often nearby.

bluegill

crappie

walleye

pike

muskellunge

Freshwater Giant

The white sturgeon is the largest freshwater fish in North America. This enormous fish can grow to be 20 feet (6 meters) long and weigh more than 1,700 pounds (770 kilograms).

white sturgeon

9

FISHING TACKLE

Fishing equipment is called tackle. Anglers need rods, **reels**, fishing line, and hooks. Fishing rods are made of strong, flexible materials such as **carbon fiber** or **fiberglass**. Most rods are between 5 and 7 feet (1.5 and 2.1 meters) long. Anglers turn reels to bring in the fishing line. They choose line based on the size of fish they want to catch. For heavier fish, they need stronger, thicker line.

Anglers have a couple of options to attract fish. Some put **live bait** on their hooks and **bobbers** on their lines. When a fish bites the bait, it also bites the hook and pulls the bobber underwater. Other anglers use **lures** to draw in fish. Lures are made of metal, plastic, or wood. They are shiny, colorful, and designed to look and move like baitfish.

Alluring Names

Lures come in many styles and often have unusual names. Some of the most common types of lures are poppers, spinners, jigs, and plugs.

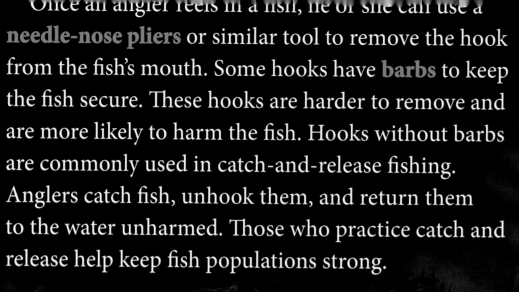

needle-nose pliers or similar tool to remove the hook from the fish's mouth. Some hooks have barbs to keep the fish secure. These hooks are harder to remove and are more likely to harm the fish. Hooks without barbs are commonly used in catch-and-release fishing. Anglers catch fish, unhook them, and return them to the water unharmed. Those who practice catch and release help keep fish populations strong.

Make It Snappy

Anglers who practice catch and release must get the fish back into the water as quickly as possible. They should also be careful not to damage the slime coating on the fish as they remove the hook.

needle-nose
pliers

RESPECT AND SAFETY

Responsible anglers take pride in protecting the waters where they fish. Clean habitats help fish stay safe and healthy. Anglers would not want to eat fish that came from polluted waters!

Anglers should never throw any trash into the water. This includes used fishing line and hooks, which harm fish and birds. They should also pick up litter left behind by others. Anglers must remember to clean the outsides of their boats after trips. This prevents them from transporting **invasive species** to other lakes and rivers.

Showing courtesy to others is an important part of freshwater fishing. Anglers must stay off private land and remain quiet on the water. They should drive their boats slowly and keep their distance when others are fishing nearby.

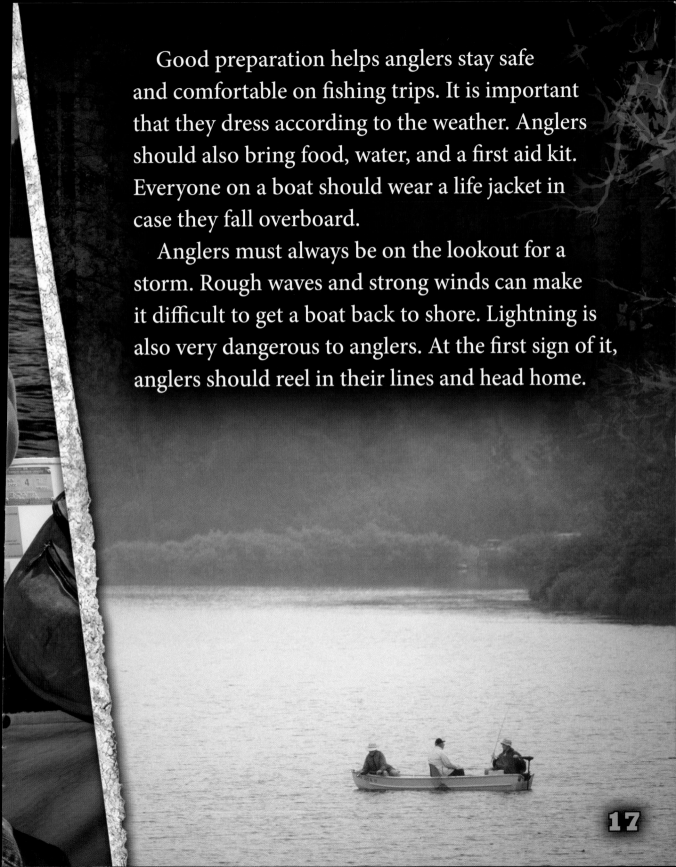

Good preparation helps anglers stay safe and comfortable on fishing trips. It is important that they dress according to the weather. Anglers should also bring food, water, and a first aid kit. Everyone on a boat should wear a life jacket in case they fall overboard.

Anglers must always be on the lookout for a storm. Rough waves and strong winds can make it difficult to get a boat back to shore. Lightning is also very dangerous to anglers. At the first sign of it, anglers should reel in their lines and head home.

Each state has fishing rules that all anglers must follow. They determine the types, sizes, and numbers of fish that can be kept. They also list the places where people are not allowed to fish. Anglers have to buy a fishing **license** every year. They must have a license for every state where they want to fish.

These rules are in place to protect freshwater fish populations. Pollution and **overfishing** have caused many fish populations to decrease. Anglers want the fish in their lakes to continue biting for a long time!

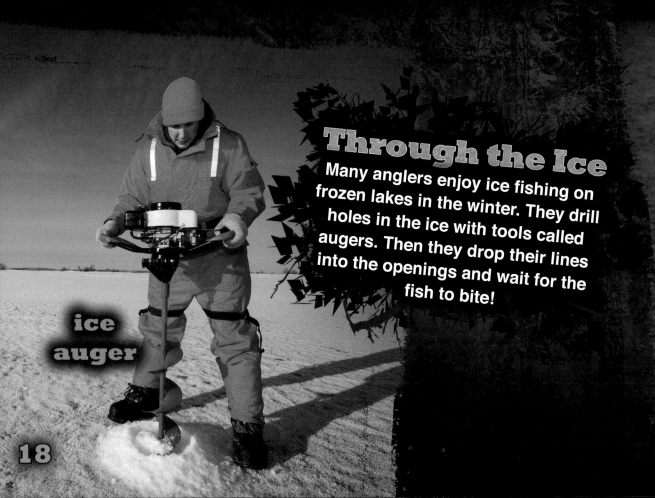

ice auger

Through the Ice

Many anglers enjoy ice fishing on frozen lakes in the winter. They drill holes in the ice with tools called augers. Then they drop their lines into the openings and wait for the fish to bite!

MINNESOTA: LAND OF 10,000 LAKES

With more than 10,000 lakes, Minnesota draws anglers from all over the country. Walleye, pike, catfish, bass, and perch are among the many types of fish found in Minnesota's lakes.

Lake of the Woods is especially famous for its fishing. The lake is located in northern Minnesota and crosses into Canada. It is the sixth largest freshwater lake in the United States. It contains more than 14,500 islands and has 65,000 miles (104,600 kilometers) of shoreline. Many kinds of fish are caught in Lake of the Woods, but walleye and trout are the most abundant. Anglers may spot bears, otters, and bald eagles around the lake. The natural beauty and rewarding catches make Lake of the Woods a perfect freshwater fishing destination.

Lake of
the Woods

GLOSSARY

angler—a person who fishes

baitfish—small fish that attract game fish

barbs—sharp points on some fishing hooks; barbs make it easier for a hook to stay in a fish's mouth.

bobbers—small floats placed on fishing lines

carbon fiber—a strong, flexible material made by weaving threads of carbon together

casts—throws fishing line out into the water

fiberglass—a strong, lightweight material made by weaving threads of glass together

freshwater—water with little to no salt; lakes, ponds, rivers, and streams contain freshwater.

game fish—fish caught for sport

invasive species—animals and plants that are not originally from an area and are likely to harm the area

landing—bringing onto land or into a boat

license—a document that gives legal permission to do an activity

live bait—bait that an angler puts on a hook to attract fish; worms, leeches, and minnows are commonly used as live bait.

lures—shiny, colorful pieces of fishing equipment that anglers use to attract fish

needle-nose pliers—a tool with a narrow head used for gripping; anglers use needle-nose pliers to remove hooks from the mouths of fish.

overfishing—greatly reducing the number of fish in an area by fishing too much

reels—devices that allow anglers to pull in and let out fishing line

sets the hook—firmly secures a hook in a fish's mouth by jerking the fishing rod

TO LEARN MORE

At the Library

Lindeen, Carol K. *Freshwater Fishing*. Mankato, Minn.: Capstone Press, 2011.

Schwartz, Tina. *Freshwater Fishing*. New York, N.Y.: PowerKids Press, 2012.

Seeberg, Tim. *Freshwater Fishing*. Chanhassen, Minn.: Child's World, 2004.

On the Web

Learning more about freshwater fishing is as easy as 1, 2, 3.

1. Go to www.factsurfer.com.

2. Enter "freshwater fishing" into the search box.

3. Click the "Surf" button and you will see a list of related Web sites.

With factsurfer.com, finding more information is just a click away.

INDEX